PIANO • VOCAL • GUITAR

BROADWAY COMEDY SONGS

ISBN 0-7935-2690-6

A Joint Publication of
MPL COMMUNICATIONS, INC.
and
HB® Hal Leonard Publishing Corporation

Exclusively Distributed by
HB® Hal Leonard Publishing Corporation
7777 West Bluemound Road P.O. Box 13819 Milwaukee, WI 53213

BROADWAY

COMEDY SONGS

ALONE AT THE DRIVE-IN MOVIE

from GREASE

Lyric and Music by
WARREN CASEY and JIM JACOBS

6

lights go down low, I'll be hold-ing the speak-er knobs, miss-ing you

so._____ I can't be-lieve_ it,_____

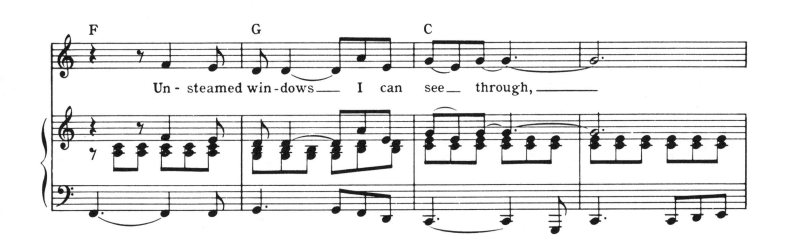

Un-steamed win-dows_ I can see_ through,_____

Might as well be in an ig - loo, _____

'Cause the heat - er does-n't work as good as

you. _____ (Ba - by come back.)

CLEOPATTERER

from LEAVE IT TO JANE

Words and Music by JEROME KERN
and P.G. WODEHOUSE

10

COME ALONG WITH ME

from CAN-CAN

Words and Music by
COLE PORTER

13

DANCE: TEN; LOOKS: THREE

from A CHORUS LINE

Music by MARVIN HAMLISCH
Lyric by EDWARD KLEBAN

DOWN IN THE DEPTHS
(ON THE NINETIETH FLOOR)

from RED, HOT AND BLUE!

Words and Music by
COLE PORTER

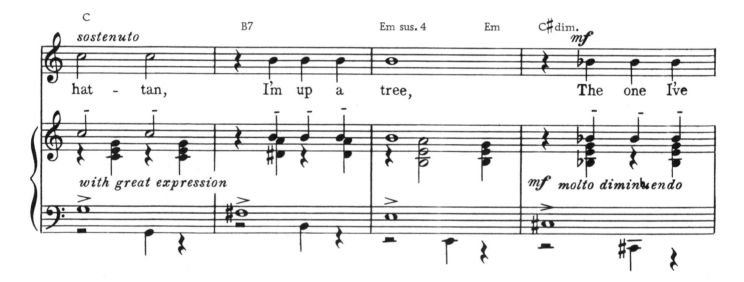

23

24

26

DISGUSTINGLY RICH

from HIGHER AND HIGHER

Lyrics by LORENZ HART
Music by RICHARD RODGERS

IT'S A LOVELY DAY FOR A MURDER

from HIGHER AND HIGHER

Lyrics by LORENZ HART
Music by RICHARD RODGERS

Moderately Bright

Have you ev - er heard of Saint Bar - thol - o - mew's Day?
Or the day when we have our tax - es to pay?

Or the day when they
Or the day when the

took our li - quor a - way?
Tro - jans were fooled by U -

HAPPY TO KEEP HIS DINNER WARM

from HOW TO SUCCEED IN BUSINESS WITHOUT REALLY TRYING

By FRANK LOESSER

I WANT TO BE BAD

from GOOD NEWS

Words and Music by B.G. DESYLVA,
LEW BROWN and RAY HENDERSON

44

I WISH I WERE IN LOVE AGAIN

from BABES IN ARMS

Words by LORENZ HART
Music by RICHARD RODGERS

I'M CALM

from A FUNNY THING HAPPENED ON THE WAY TO THE FORUM

Words and Music by
STEPHEN SONDHEIM

Em - er - ald rings. Or a mur - mur - ing

brook _ _ Mur - mur - ing, mur - mur - ing, mur - mur - ing _ _ Look: I'm

calm, I'm calm, I have-n't a qualm. I'm ut - ter - ly un - der con -

trol. _ _ _ _ _ Let noth - ing con - fuse me, or faze me _ _ Ex -

IT AIN'T ETIQUETTE
from DUBARRY WAS A LADY

Words and Music by
COLE PORTER

JOHNNY ONE NOTE

from BABES IN ARMS

Words by LORENZ HART
Music by RICHARD RODGERS

NELSON
from A DAY IN HOLLYWOOD

Music and Lyric by
JERRY HERMAN

Rubato

Bb   Gm

My heart,   my love, my life is his a - lone.   But

Eb   Cm   F7sus4   F7

if,   but if, but if the truth be known.

64

not hard to sleep through it all. _____ His vo - cal chords
mer - i - ca's sweet-hearts my ass. _____ "A pair made in

car - ry in - sur - ance by Lloyd's and so, might I add, should
heav - en," the fans love to say, and but each time we kiss I

his ad - e - noids. The lights wilt his hair - do on cam - era he'll
swear that he's gay. In film af - ter film af - ter film I be -

primp and quite frank - ly, his hair is - n't all that goes limp. Dar - ling
trothed him, we snug - gled and smooched, and oh God, how I loathed him. My

LET'S NOT TALK ABOUT LOVE
from LET'S FACE IT

Words and Music by
COLE PORTER

70

72

love. Let's talk a - bout drugs, Let's talk a-bout dope, Let's try to pic-ture Par-a-mount

mi - nus Bob Hope, Let's start a new dance, Let's try a new step, Or in-

ves - ti-gate the cause of Mis-sus Roos-e-velt's pep, Why not dis-cuss, my dee-a-rie, The

life of Wal-lace Bee-a-ry, Or bring a jer-o-bo-am on And write a drunk-en po-em on Ti-

A LITTLE MORE MASCARA

from LA CAGE AUX FOLLES

Music and Lyric by
JERRY HERMAN

Once a-gain, I'm a lit-tle de-pressed by the tired old face that I see; Once a-gain, it is time to be some-one, who's an-y-one oth-er than me. With a rare com-bi-na-tion of girl-ish ex-cite-ment and man-ly re-straint, I po-

A LITTLE RUMBA NUMBA
from LET'S FACE IT

Words and Music by
COLE PORTER

A lit-tle rum - ba num - ba   Down Ar-gen-ti - na way,

Made me for get   to slum - ba,   As through a dance she'd sway,   Sing-ing

LOOK AT ME, I'M SANDRA DEE

from GREASE

Lyric and Music by
WARREN CASEY and JIM JACOBS

Sung an octave lower than written

88

NOBODY MAKES A PASS AT ME

from PINS AND NEEDLES

Words and Music by
HAROLD ROME

No - bo - dy makes a pass at me! I'm full of Kell-ogg's bran, eat
No - bo - dy makes a pass at me! I use Pond's on my skin, with

grape-nuts on the sly, A date is on the can of the cof - fee that I buy
rye - crisp I have thinned, I get my cul-ture in I be - gan "Gone With The Wind"

Oh dear, what can the mat - ter be? No - bo - dy makes a pass at me!
Oh dear, what can the mat - ter be? No - bo - dy makes a pass at me!

Oh Bea-trice Fair-fax, give me the bare facts, How do you make them fall?
Oh Dor - 'thy Dix, please, show me some tricks, please, I want some men to hold.

94

PATTER

SALZBURG
from BELLS ARE RINGING

Words by BETTY COMDEN and ADOLPH GREEN
Music by JULE STYNE

Bright Waltz *(In 1)*

98

PUSH DE BUTTON
from JAMAICA

Lyric by E.Y. HARBURG
Music by HAROLD ARLEN

102

SHE DIDN'T SAY "YES"

from THE CAT AND THE FIDDLE

Words and Music by
JEROME KERN

106

SIBERIA
from SILK STOCKINGS

Words and Music by
COLE PORTER

*Superia meaning Superior.

110

SING ME A SONG WITH SOCIAL SIGNIFICANCE

from PINS AND NEEDLES

Words and Music by
HAROLD ROME

THAT'LL SHOW HIM
from A FUNNY THING HAPPENED ON THE WAY TO THE FORUM

Words and Music by
STEPHEN SONDHEIM

Our re - venge will start! _____

When I kiss him, I'll be kiss - ing you.

So I'll kiss him morn - ing and night... That - 'll show him!

When I hold him, I'll be hold - ing you,

So I'll hold him ten times as tight.. That-'ll show him too! ____

I shall coo and ten-der-ly stroke his

hair.. Wish that you were there..

You'd en-joy it! When it's eve-ning And we're in our

TRIPLETS
from BETWEEN THE DEVIL

Words by HOWARD DIETZ
Music by ARTHUR SCHWARTZ

122

Patter

TAKE BACK YOUR MINK
from GUYS AND DOLLS

By FRANK LOESSER

* Symbols for Guitar, Diagrams for Ukulele.

WHERE, OH WHERE

from OUT OF THIS WORLD

Words and Music by
COLE PORTER

WELL, DID YOU EVAH?
from DUBARRY WAS A LADY

Words and Music by
COLE PORTER

WELL, DID YOU EVAH?

REFRAIN 1

She: Have you heard the coast of Maine
  Just got hit by a hurricane?
He: Well, did you evah! What a swell party this is.
She: Have you heard that poor, dear Blanche
  Got run down by an avalanche?
He: Well, did you evah! What a swell party this is.
  It's great, it's grand.
  It's Wonderland!
  It's tops, it's first.
  It's DuPont, it's Hearst!
  What soup, what fish.
  That meat, what a dish!
  What salad, what cheese!
She: Pardon me one moment, please,
  Have you heard that Uncle Newt
  Forgot to open his parachute?
He: Well, did you evah! What a swell party this is.
She: Old Aunt Susie just came back
  With her child and the child is black.
He: Well, did you evah! What a swell party this is.

REFRAIN 2

He: Have you heard it's in the stars
  Next July we collide with Mars?
She: Well, did you evah! What a swell party this is.
He: Have you heard that Grandma Doyle
  Thought the Flit was her mineral oil?
She: Well, did you evah! What a swell party this is.
  What Daiquiris!
  What Sherry! Please!
  What Burgundy!
  What great Pommery!
  What brandy, wow!
  What whiskey, here's how!
  What gin and what beer!
He: Will you sober up, my dear?
  Have you heard Professor Munch
  Ate his wife and divorced his lunch?
She: Well, did you evah! What a swell party this is.
He: Have you heard that Mimmsie Starr
  Just got pinched in the Astor Bar?
She: Well, did you evah! What a swell party this is!

REFRAIN 3

She: Have you heard that poor old Ted
  Just turned up in an oyster bed?
He: Well, did you evah! What a swell party this is.
She: Lilly Lane has louzy luck,
  She was there when the light'ning struck.
He: Well, did you evah! What a swell party this is.
  It's fun, it's fine,
  It's too divine.
  It's smooth, it's smart.
  It's Rodgers, it's Hart!
  What debs, what stags.
  What gossip, what gags!
  What feathers, what fuss!
She: Just between the two of us,
  Reggie's rather scatterbrained,
  He dove in when the pool was drained.
He: Well, did you evah! What a swell party this is.
She: Mrs. Smith in her new Hup
  Crossed the bridge when the bridge was up.
He: Well, did you evah! What a swell party this is!

He: Have you heard that Mrs. Cass
  Had three beers and then ate the glass?
She: Well, did you evah! What a swell party this is.
He: Have you heard that Captain Craig
  Breeds termites in his wooden leg?

Ethel Merman, Bert Lahr in DuBARRY WAS A LADY (1939)

She: Well, did you evah! What a swell party this is.
  It's fun, it's fresh.
  It's post depresh.
  It's Shangrilah.
  It's Harper's Bazaar!
  What clothes, quel chic,
  What pearls, they're the peak!
  What glamour, what cheer!
He: This will simply slay you dear,
  Kitty isn't paying calls,
  She slipped over Niagara Falls.
She: Well, did you evah! What a swell party this is.
He: Have you heard that Mayor Hague
  Just came down with bubonic plague?
She: Well, did you evah! What a swell party this is.

YOUR FEET'S TOO BIG

from AIN'T MISBEHAVIN'

Words and Music by
ADA BENSON and FRED FISHER

WHY DO THE WRONG PEOPLE TRAVEL?

from SAIL AWAY

Words and Music by
NOËL COWARD

142

144